The MESSY BOOK

OF THINGS TO MAKE AND DO

by **GILLIAN OSBAND**

illustrated by **HEATHER MUNRO**

D0874335

SCHOLASTIC INC.
New York Toronto London Auckland Sydney

No part of this publication may be reproduced
in whole or in part, or stored in a retrieval
system, or transmitted in any form or by any means,
electronic, mechanical, photocopying, recording,
or otherwise, without written permission of
the publisher. For information regarding permission, write to
Scholastic Inc., 730 Broadway, New York, NY 10003.

ISBN 0-590-40888-7

First published by Scholastic Publications Ltd., 1986.
Copyright © Manor Lodge Productions Limited, 1986. All rights reserved.
Published by Scholastic Inc., by arrangement with Scholastic Publications Ltd.,
10 Earlham Street, London WC2H 9LN, United Kingdom.

12 11 10 9 8 7 6 5 4 3 2   1 2 3/9

Printed in the U.S.A.   08
First Scholastic printing, December 1987

contents

READ THIS FIRST:

★ Before you start, read all the instructions carefully. If there is anything you do not understand, **ASK FOR HELP**.

★ Read all the warnings carefully. You do not want to find that you have made so much mess all around you that you are not allowed to make messy things again!

★ Collect all the things you need before you begin. If you get stuck – **ASK FOR HELP**

MESSY RACES

drink up

Each racer needs: a plastic cup full of water.

This race is best done **OUTSIDE.**

See who can drink ALL the water first BUT – you have to drink from the edge FARTHEST AWAY from you without spilling a drop!

If you spill anything – you're **OUT!**

slurp

Each slurper needs: a bowl of ice cream (same amount for each slurper); and a straw.

See who can finish the ice cream first. . .BUT. . .you can **ONLY** use your straw to eat it!

Slurpy Tip: Let your ice cream melt and then suck it up.

duck for doughnuts

You Need:
- ★ A doughnut for each racer;
- ★ A long piece of string tied between two chair backs, or between a doorknob and a chair;
- ★ A piece of clean string (about 24 inches long) for each doughnut.

Thread a piece of string through each doughnut and tie it.

Tie each doughnut to the long line between the two chairs.

Each racer has to eat the dangling doughnut **WITHOUT** touching it with his or her hands and **WITHOUT** the doughnut falling off the string.

If you touch it – or if it falls off – you're OUT.

Who can eat a jelly doughnut **WITHOUT** licking his or her lips – or fingers – OR getting jelly on his or her fingers?

BLOWING BUBBLES

You Need:
★ Dishwashing liquid
★ A bowl
★ Water
★ A key ring or
★ A curtain ring
★ A sieve or a loop earring . . . anything with a hole in it!

What you do:

1. Squirt some dishwashing liquid in the bowl. Add a little water. Stir it with your fingers to make it nice and soapy.

2. Dip the holey things in the soapy water and . . .
BLOW BUBBLES!

What different shapes can you get?

Which shapes make the best bubbles?

Who can make the biggest bubbles?

How long can you keep your bubbles in the air by blowing them?

CAN YOU BLOW A BUBBLE WITH BUBBLE GUM? IF YOU PRACTICE YOU MAY BE ABLE TO BEAT THE WORLD RECORD FOR THE BIGGEST BUBBLE EVER. IT WAS 22 INCHES IN DIAMETER AND BLOWN BY MRS. SUSAN MONTGOMERY WILLIAMS OF FRESNO, CA, IN 1985.

LET'S BE MESSY WITH PAINTS

bubble bursts

Before you start:

COVER EVERYTHING NEAR YOU WITH NEWSPAPER

You Need:
★ Dishwashing liquid
★ Water ★ Paints
★ A pitcher
★ Clean, empty yogurt containers
★ Straws ★ Paper
★ Scissors

What you do:

1. Squirt the dishwashing liquid in the pitcher, and then fill it with water.

2. Put a different color paint in each yogurt container – and then fill the container half-full with soapy water.

3. Fray the end of the straw by making small cuts at one end and pushing them back like this:

4. Dip the end of the straw in a paint pot – and blow it at the paper. You will get wonderful bubble bursts! Try it with different colors – and practice getting your bubble to burst where you want it! You may prefer to use a different straw for each color.

See what happens when you blow for a short time – and a long time. You will have to practice to see how much paint you need on the end of the straw.

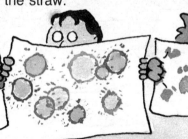

REMEMBER:

You can be messy.
The painting can be messy.
BUT – NOTHING ELSE MUST HAVE ANY PAINT ON IT!

Your picture can be lots of different bubble bursts, OR you can make your bubble bursts into flowers, animals, or strange creatures!

splatter pictures

You Need:
★ Some old toothbrushes
★ Paper ★ Paints
★ Old saucers or small bowls

What you do:

1. Put a different-colored paint in each saucer. Keep a couple of saucers for mixing colors. If the paint is very thick, you will need to add a little water.

2. Dip a toothbrush in the paint. (Use a different toothbrush for each color.) Then run your fingers along the bristles toward you, with the brush aimed at the paper. The paint will SPLATTER on the paper.

Splatter different colors until you have decided there are enough splatters on the paper.

If you want only one area splattered, or want a splatter border, cover the area you want to keep clean with paper or newspaper before you start.

SPLATTER PAPER makes nice wrapping paper – or tape it around a notebook to make a nice cover.

You can also put leaves or cutout paper shapes on the paper before you splatter. When you lift them off, the shape will be left white.

Hot tip: You can use a ruler instead of your finger.

dribbling

This can be **VERY MESSY** – so make **DOUBLE** sure that **EVERYTHING ELSE IS COVERED!**

You Need:
★ Several clean, empty yogurt containers.
★ Paints ★ Paper
★ Water ★ A straw
★ Your fingers

What you do:

1. Put a different-colored paint in each container and add enough water to make the paint thick but still runny.

2. Pour a little of the paint onto the paper, moving the container so that the paint DRIBBLES.

3. Dribble different colors.

4. You can also dip your fingers in the paint and let the paint drip onto the paper.

5. Then to spread the paint in odd swirls and patterns, **BLOW** at it through the straw.

Another idea. . .dip an old sponge in the paint and dab it on the paper to make textured pictures.

YOU ARE THE PAINTBRUSH

Using your fingers; thumb; side of your hand; fist and your palm, you can paint wonderful pictures, and only YOU will be messy!

You Need:
- ★ Poster paints
- ★ Water
- ★ A paint brush
- ★ Several old saucers or small bowls
- ★ Paper for your pictures
- ★ A rag
- ★ Your hand

What you do:

1. Put a different-colored paint in each saucer. Keep a couple of saucers for mixing colors.

2. Here are some things you can copy to see how they were done. Then try some on your own.

PAINT THE EYES, BEAK AND FEET

SIDE OF YOUR HAND

SIDE OF YOUR LITTLE FINGER

To Get The Best Pictures:

Use paint that is just sticky. You won't get a clear print if it is too wet.

Dab your fingers, fist etc, in the paint – and then press gently onto the paper.

You will know if the paint is the right stickiness because you will be able to see the swirls and lines on your finger tips.

Before you begin your pictures, see what shapes you get from the different parts of your hand. Try rolling your fingers, fist, etc., to see what shape that makes.

LOTS OF FINGER PRINTS

THUMB PRINT

Either you can make your whole picture from your prints – or you can paint in details like eyes, wheel spokes, and bird feet, with a paint brush.

You could also have a **SPLATTER BORDER** around your picture.

LITTLE FINGER PRINTS

WHY DID THE ELEPHANT PAINT HIMSELF DIFFERENT COLORS?

SO HE COULD HIDE IN THE PAINTBOX!

MESSY GAMES

ball**oo**n balls

Two or more players.

This game **MUST BE PLAYED OUT-SIDE** and is best played on a hot, sunny day.

You Need: ★ Some large balloons
                ★ Water

Fill your balloons with water.

Then carefully tie a knot at the end. Be careful you don't squirt the water all over you!

You now have squelchy balloon balls!

BALLOON BALLS are strong as long as you don't drop them or prick them.

Take one ball and throw it from player to player. As long as the balloon ball is caught it shouldn't burst! If you drop it you will probably get wet!

How long can you keep the ball in the air?

Who stays driest longest?

IT'S AMAZING!

QUEEN ELIZABETH I WAS THOUGHT TO BE VERY CLEAN BY EVERYONE AT COURT BECAUSE SHE TOOK A BATH **ONCE A MONTH!**

HOW DO ELEPHANTS GET IN THE BATH?

THEY TAKE THEIR TRUNKS OFF!

eat your breakfast *BLINDFOLDED*

You will have to ask your parents before you do this since you will probably make an awful mess at the breakfast table. Don't try it on a school day either!

Have you ever thought about how lucky you are to be able to see?

NOW: ask one family member to blindfold you with a scarf.

THEN: find your way to the table and eat your breakfast with the blindfold on!

Put cereal in your bowl and pour milk on it. Find the spoon and get the cereal and milk from the bowl to your mouth.

Find the butter and jam and put them on your toast. Pour yourself a drink – will you find the glass?

You can ask the rest of the family to give you instructions.

How much do you now use your sense of hearing, smell, and touch?

BET YOU CAN'T. . .

Can you eat a bowl of your favorite soup . . .**WITH A FORK?**

Can you drink your soup using the smallest spoon you can find – and **WITHOUT LETTING ANY OF IT DROP OFF THE SPOON?**

Can you eat crackers or cookies with a KNIFE AND FORK – and **WITHOUT** touching them with your fingers?

flour cake walk

Any number can play.

What you do:

1. Put newspaper on a table and on the floor.

2. Fill a dish with a large mound of flour. Then put a small apple, a nut or a candy on top of the mound.

3. Place the dish on the paper-covered table or on the floor. Put a spoon and an empty bowl next to the dish.

4. Get a radio, or a tape player and a cassette with music.

How to play:

1. Choose someone to start and stop the music. While the music is playing, the players walk around the table (or the dish on the floor).

2. When the music stops, whoever is nearest the spoon must scoop away a spoonful of flour **WITHOUT** dislodging the apple/nut/candy. Put the spoon of flour in the bowl.

3. When the apple/nut/candy falls, the unlucky player must get it out with his or her teeth and put it back in the middle. If it falls near the middle, you can get covered with flour!!!

apple bobbing

This is a very old, traditional game that was often played at Halloween.

You can get nice and wet. . .

All you need are some small apples and a clean bucket or bowl of water.

Put the apples in the bucket of water. They will bob around.

Each player has to try to get an apple out of the water using **ONLY HIS OR HER TEETH!** Give each player one minute (or perhaps two) to get the apple out.

MESSY IN THE KITCHEN

Although you will end up with **MESSY** hands, make sure they are **CLEAN** when you start!!!

chocolate truffles

You Need:
- ★ 6 tablespoons of powdered cocoa
- ★ 2 tablespoons of confectioners' sugar
- ★ ¼ cup of soft butter (take it out of the refrigerator half an hour before you need it) ★ A bowl

1. Put everything in the bowl. Hold the bowl with one hand.

2. Knead the mixture together with the other until it is well mixed.

3. Roll the mixture into little balls. Put some cocoa powder on a plate. Roll the balls in the powder to cover them.

TERR-UFFICLE!

Humpty Dumpty sat on a wall,
Humpty Dumpty had a great fall,
All the King's horses and all the King's men,
Had scrambled eggs for dinner again!

super sandwiches

Sandwiches can be BORING. . .or they can be gooey and scrumptious!

Butter two slices of bread, or three if you are going to have a double decker. Then try one of these mixtures.

HONEY, PEANUTS AND MASHED BANANA

CAN YOU EAT A PACKAGE OF POTATO CHIPS WITHOUT LICKING YOUR LIPS?

PEANUT BUTTER AND m&m's

COLD BREAKFAST SAUSAGES AND STRAWBERRY JAM

HARD-BOILED EGG, POTATO CHIPS AND DEVILED HAM

funny faces

You can make **FUNNY FACES** on cupcakes or on plain sugar cookies.

You Need: ★ A box of confectioners' sugar
★ Food coloring
★ 3 or 4 small bowls
★ A frosting squeezer
★ A large bowl
★ A wooden spoon
★ A blunt knife

1. Put half the box of confectioners' sugar in the big bowl. Add water, a few drops at a time, and stir until you have a thick paste.

2. Put some of the sugar paste in each small bowl. Add a few drops of food coloring (one to each bowl) and mix it so that in each bowl you have a different-colored icing.

3. Choose a color and spread it over the top of the cupcakes or cookies with the blunt knife.

4. Put one color in the frosting squeezer, and make hair. Squeeze whatever is left in the squeezer back into the bowl, and wash out the top.

5. Put in another color for the eyes, the nose and the mouth.

Here are some faces to copy. You can also use candies for the eyes, nose and mouth.

YUM! YUM!

MUSHY PAPER MODELING

You can make model cats, dogs, rockets, cars, cakes – even a head – all from. . .

★ Old newspapers
★ Flour
★ and water

You also need a large, old bowl.

If you need any help – **ASK!**

What you do:

1. Put about 10 tablespoons of flour in the bowl. Slowly add some water and stir until you have made a gooey paste.

2. Tear up some of the newspapers into pieces about an inch square. Put them in the bowl with the paste.

3. Let the newspapers soak in the paste for a while. Then stir. When the mixture becomes a gray doughy mess, it's ready. If it looks too dry, add a little more water. If it is too runny, add a little more paper.

This is called papier maché.

4. Take a lump of the mixture. If you can, work on a hard surface that can be wiped clean.

You will be able to push and squeeze the papier maché into any shape you want. You can add extra bits for heads, legs or whatever you need.

5. When you have made your cat or house or apple, tear up some small pieces of newspaper.

Cover your model with these dry pieces of paper. They will stick to it because of the paste in the papier mâché

6. Leave it somewhere warm to dry. It will take 3 days, but your model will then be as hard as a rock.

Why don't you make papier mâché cupcakes? Decorate them, put them on a plate and see if you can fool everyone into thinking they're real!

7. If you want to, you can paint your model. When the paint is dry, you can varnish with egg white.

IT'S AMAZING!

WATER IS QUITE EXTRAORDINARY!
IT IS MADE UP OF TWO GASES WHICH HAVE
JOINED TOGETHER TO MAKE A LIQUID

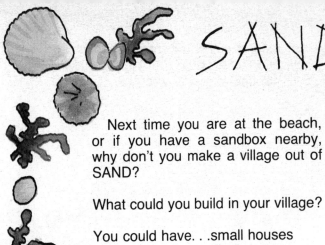

SAND PLAY

Next time you are at the beach, or if you have a sandbox nearby, why don't you make a village out of SAND?

What could you build in your village?

You could have. . .small houses
big houses
shops
a church
gardens
roads
cars
a village green
with a pond

Are your houses going to be along a road or around a village green?

Are the gardens going to have pebble walls or twig hedges – or both?

Your houses can be tall or small. They can be square or L-shaped, or long and narrow.

If you are building in a sandbox, you will need a bucket of water to make the sand wet, or you will have to wait until it has rained. Otherwise your village won't stay up!

If you are on the beach, build in the wet sand.

Collect: pebbles; shells; twigs; leaves; seaweed.

Use pebbles and shells to mark the doors and windows. You can also use them for walls and for the roofs.

Use leaves, seaweed and twigs for the gardens, for the hedges or for trees along the road.

Use the twigs to mark out shapes on your houses and shops or on the pavement and roads.

You can make sand cars and trucks to go along the road, or you can use toys.

Can you make a seat by the pond?

Look at the village here which shows you how to make the basic shapes.

21

TERRIBLE TRICKS

a trick messy trick

You: I bet you I can stay under water for 5 minutes.

Victim: *I bet you can't!*

You: I bet you three chocolate bars that I can.

Victim: *Okay, it's a bet . . . you can't do it!*

Get a glass of water and hold it over your head for 5 minutes! You've won your bet. You have stayed UNDER WATER FOR 5 MINUTES

You may, of course, get water thrown at you. . .

it's raining cats and dogs

You need:
- ★ An umbrella
- ★ Old newspaper or magazine.

Tear the magazine or newspaper into lots of small pieces.

Open the umbrella a little bit, and drop all the pieces of paper into it.

Next time it rains, whoever uses the umbrella will find it's raining. . .paper!

Don't forget about your trick or your victim may be. . .YOU!

You will need to make yourself invisible when it works; otherwise you will have to clean it all up!

jam shake

Choose your victim.

Put a spoonful of strawberry jam on the palm of your right hand. Bend your fingers over so that the jam can't be seen.

Go up to your victim and say you want to shake hands to congratulate him on being the best runner you know, or the worst joke teller ever, or. . . . You can think of something!

Shake hands. . .and run!

WHY? You have covered his hand with strawberry jam!

make a trick bottle

You Need: ★ An empty, plastic bottle with a screw top
★ A pin
★ Water
★ A victim!

Make several tiny holes in the bottom of the bottle with the pin.

Then fill the bottle by putting it in a sink that's full of water. You will know when the bottle is full because no more air bubbles will come out of it. With the bottle still **under the water,** screw on the top.

Take the bottle out and wipe it dry. No water will come out of the bottom.

Tell your victim you can't undo the top. When she unscrews it for you, she will get a fountain all over her feet from the pinholes!

Be prepared to run!

a trick drinking straw

Make **tiny** holes around the straw, with the pin. Get a drink for your victim and yourself.

Give your victim the trick straw – and put a normal one in your drink. When he drinks he won't be able to understand why he is getting wet!!!

YUK!

You Need: ★ A brown bag
           ★ A plastic bag
           ★ A grape, or a damp
              sponge, or a raw
              sausage
           ★ Tape

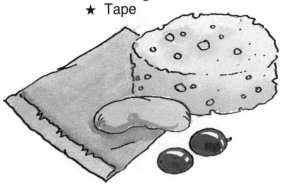

Put the plastic bag inside the brown bag to make it waterproof. Put the grape, the damp sponge, or the raw sausage in the bag. Tape the top of the bag so that the hole is only big enough to put a hand through.

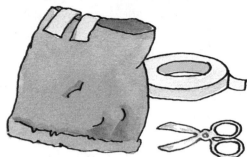

You: You'll never guess what I've got in this bag.

Victim: *I've no idea. What is it?*

You: A giant's eye. . .or a dragon's brain. . .or a witch's finger (it depends on what you've got in there).

Victim: *I don't believe you!*

You: Put your hand in and feel.

                  Victim: *Yuk!!!!*

You can also ask your victim to put his hand in the bag and guess what is inside – and then tell him it's a giant's eye.

PUDDLE FUN

Splashing. . .

Put on your rubber boots and see who can make the biggest splash! Take turns jumping in the middle of puddles with both feet.

Hopping. . .

Can you hop over the puddles without getting your feet wet?

How many times can you hop backward and forward without putting your foot down – and without landing in the puddle?

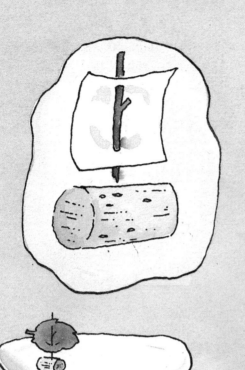

Racing. . .

Race cork boats across your puddle.

All you need are some corks, small sticks, and some paper or large leaves.

Put them on the edge of the puddle and blow them across.

Either have races with a friend, or see how quickly you can blow your boat across.

You don't have to wait for the weather to be wet to have cork boat races. You can fill a basin with water. If you do race the boats inside, put paper on the floor around you!!

Floating. . .

Gather together lots of different things like:

    pebbles
    grass
    a leaf
    a twig
    a piece of paper
    a cork
    a lollipop
– and drop them in your puddle.

What happens to them?

Do they sink? Do they float?

Do they float for a while and then sink?

You can also try this game with a bowl of water indoors.

HOW MUCH MUD IS THERE IN A HOLE: 14 inches DEEP, 24 inches WIDE AND 24 inches WIDE.

NONE!

DRESSING UP

READ THIS FIRST!

When you put on makeup, you must **ONLY USE:**

★ Q-tips
★ Children's body paints
★ Your mother's makeup, but ask permission first!
★ The ideas given here!

If you are going to make up your face AND your body, do it in the bathroom or the kitchen **WITH PAPER ON THE FLOOR** or do it **OUTSIDE!**

Useful things:

★ Makeup
★ An old sponge
★ Cotton balls
★ A bowl for mixing
★ Cleansing cream to remove make-up
★ Q-tips

If you are using body paints or water-based makeup, you can wash it all off.

WARNING: Do not get makeup in your eyes, in your mouth or your nose.

Look in the mirror. What can you see? Is it the same face you saw yesterday? If it is, then it's time for a change!

WOULD YOU LIKE TO BE A SKELETON?

You need:

★ Your old sponge and bowl
★ Toothpaste, white makeup or white body paint
★ An old pair of black tights

★ An old black T-shirt
★ Black eye shadow (from Mom) or a black eyebrow pencil

★ A friend to help

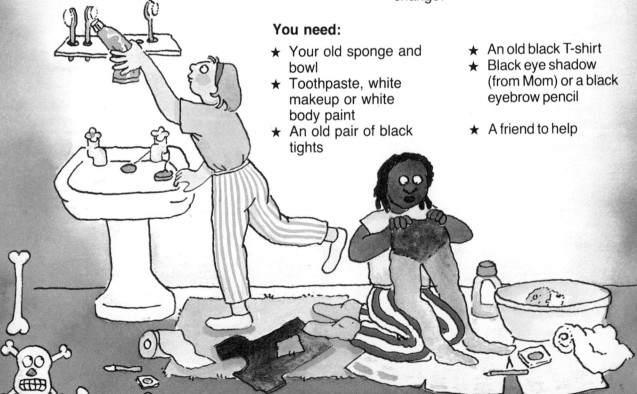

Your face:

Tie your hair back. If you can put it in a swimming cap, you will look creepier.

Use the white makeup or toothpaste mixed with a little water to make up your face like this:

Use the black eye shadow or make-up for your eyes, to shade the side of your face and to mark out your teeth.

For your body: You can feel where your main bones are. Get your friend to help you paint them on your T-shirt and tights with toothpaste, the white makeup or white body paint.

You can also paint the bones right onto your skin! You will need an old pair of shorts and if you have a light skin, black or brown body paint.

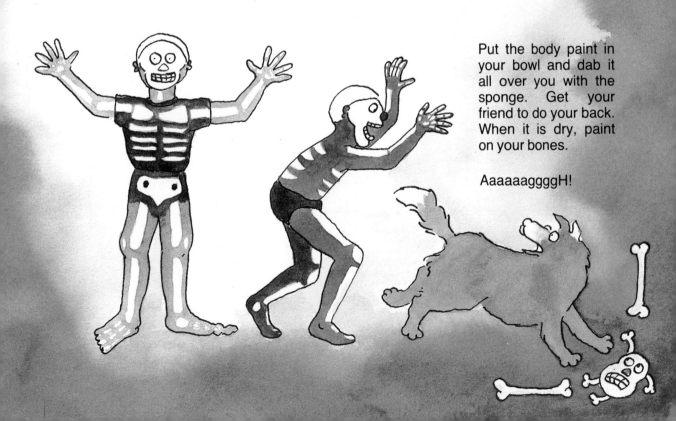

Put the body paint in your bowl and dab it all over you with the sponge. Get your friend to do your back. When it is dry, paint on your bones.

AaaaaaggggH!

AN ALIEN FROM OUTER SPACE

You Need:
★ Green body paint – or you can make a green paste by adding a little water to green eye shadow
★ An old sponge and a bowl
★ Double-sided tape
★ Aluminum foil
★ An old pair of shorts
★ A piece of wire long enough to go around your head.
★ 2 pieces of wire about 10 inches long
★ Scissors
★ A friend to help.

What you do:

1. Cut 2 pieces of aluminum foil 11 inches long, and another piece the same length as the wire to go around your head. Wrap the foil around each piece of wire. Tape the edges.

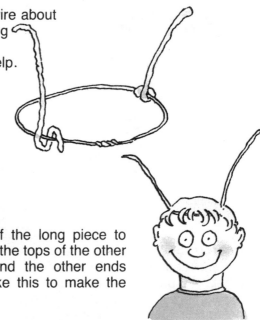

2. Join the ends of the long piece to make a circle. Bend the tops of the other 2 pieces. Then bend the other ends around the circle like this to make the antennae.

Make sure all the rough edges are covered with tape.

3. Cut out lots of aluminum-foil circles. Put double-sided tape on the back.

4. With the sponge, dab green body paint or paste over your body. Get your friend to do your back.

5. When the paint is dry, stick the aluminum-foil circles all over you – and on your cheeks and forehead.

Put on your antennae.

You can use colored tights and an old T-shirt.

Your friends can use different-colored makeup with different-colored circles so they can be extraordinary aliens, too.

If you can, paint your toenails and fingernails with nail polish of any color.

Put on a play:

Pretend you have just landed on Earth from a distant planet, very different from the Earth.

If you had never seen a flower – what would you think it was?

If you had never seen a telephone – what would you think it was?

If you had never seen a cat – would you think it was a "human"?

You can invent your own language and way of walking, too.

Do this **IN THE SINK, IN A LARGE BOWL** or **OUTSIDE!**

VOLCANO

You Need:
★ An empty, clean ink bottle or perfume bottle, or a bottle of a similar shape
★ A piece of cardboard
★ A pin
★ A small glass
★ Food coloring
★ Water

What you do:

1. Make a small hole in the middle of the cardboard with the pin.

2. Half fill the glass with cold water.

3. Put 4 or 5 drops of food coloring in the bottle. Then fill it up with **hot** water from the tap.

4. Put the cardboard over the top of the glass. Then, holding the cardboard tightly, turn the glass over onto the top of the bottle. **NO** – the water won't fall out as long as the cardboard is held firmly over the top of the glass. You may not get it right to start with and, if you spill the water, just fill the glass again.

5. As you watch, a volcano of colored water will rise into the glass.

Warm water is lighter than cold water, so the warm water rises!

THIS GAME CAN ONLY BE PLAYED OUTSIDE!!!

Any number of people can play. The more, the messier! Divide into two teams. Each team must choose a base camp and put a marker on it.

Aim: To capture the other team's camp.

Everyone in Team One Needs:
A clean, empty plastic bottle (empty dishwashing liquid bottles are good). All bottles should be about the same size, if possible. Fill them with water.

Everyone in Team Two Needs:
A paper bag full of flour.

Tip: Make sure you don't get water or flour on anyone else. They won't be too happy!!

How To Play:

Each team starts at their base camp.

One player (you have decided who before you start) yells **"SPLAT!"**

AND. . .

TEAM ONE must reach **TEAM TWO'S** base without getting any flour on them.

TEAM TWO must reach **TEAM ONE'S** base without getting wet!

If you get covered with flour or get wet, you are OUT! But you can shout to support your team.

When you run out of flour or water you just have to be VERY NIMBLE!

Whichever team ends up with the most members in the other team's camp WINS.

MOM, CAN I PLAY THE PIANO?

NOT UNTIL YOU'VE WASHED YOUR DIRTY HANDS

OH MOM, I PROMISE I'LL ONLY PLAY THE BLACK KEYS!